Ronnie Lott
GREATEST DEFENSIVE BACKS

Larry Wilson

NFL HALL OF FAMERS

GREATEST DEFENSIVE BACKS

JOE TISCHLER

Paul Krause

CREATIVE EDUCATION / CREATIVE PAPERBACKS

Published by Creative Education and Creative Paperbacks
P.O. Box 227, Mankato, Minnesota 56002
Creative Education and Creative Paperbacks
are imprints of The Creative Company
www.thecreativecompany.us

Design and production by Blue Design (www.bluedes.com)
Art direction by Rita Marshall

Images by Getty Images/Bettmann, 12, Bill Eppridge/Time Life Pictures, 7, Christian Petersen, 28, Clifton Boutelle, 3, 21, David Madison, cover, Focus On Sport, 6, 7, 22, Fred Roe, 17, George Gojkovich, 19, Gregory Shamus, 7, John Biever, 26, John Iacono, 18, Kidwiler Collection, 7, Michael Zagaris, 1, 6, Mickey Pfleger, 9, NFL/Pro Football Hall Of Fame, 6, NFL/WireImage.com, 15, Patrick Smith, 4–5, 29, 32, Peter Read Miller, 25, TIMOTHY A. CLARY, 6, Tom Dahlin, 30, Tony Tomsic, 2; Wikimedia Commons/Detroit Lions/NFL, 13, Gonzo fan2007, cover (background), public domain, 11, U.S. Coast Guard, 10

Library of Congress Cataloging-in-Publication Data
Names: Tischler, Joe, author.
Title: Greatest defensive backs / Joe Tischler.
Description: Mankato, Minnesota : Creative Education and Creative Paperbacks, [2026] | Series: Creative sports: NFL hall of famers | Includes index. | Audience: Ages 8–12 | Audience: Grades 4–6 | Summary: "Photo-driven and stat-filled, this middle-grade NFL title showcases 11 of pro football's greatest defensive backs enshrined in the Hall of Fame, from Emlen Tunnell and Dick Lane to Deion Sanders and Charles Woodson"—Provided by publisher.
Identifiers: LCCN 2024048107 (print) | LCCN 2024048108 (ebook) | ISBN 9798889896128 (library binding) | ISBN 9781682777787 (paperback) | ISBN 9798889896920 (ebook)
Subjects: LCSH: Defensive backs (Football)—United States—Biography—Juvenile literature. | Football—United States—Juvenile literature. | National Football League—Juvenile literature.
Classification: LCC GV939.A1 T53 2026 (print) | LCC GV939.A1 (ebook) | DDC 796.332092/2 [B]—dc23/eng/20231120
LC record available at https://lccn.loc.gov/2024048107
LC ebook record available at https://lccn.loc.gov/2024048108

Printed in India

Ed Reed

MOSS
81

TAYLOR
56

42

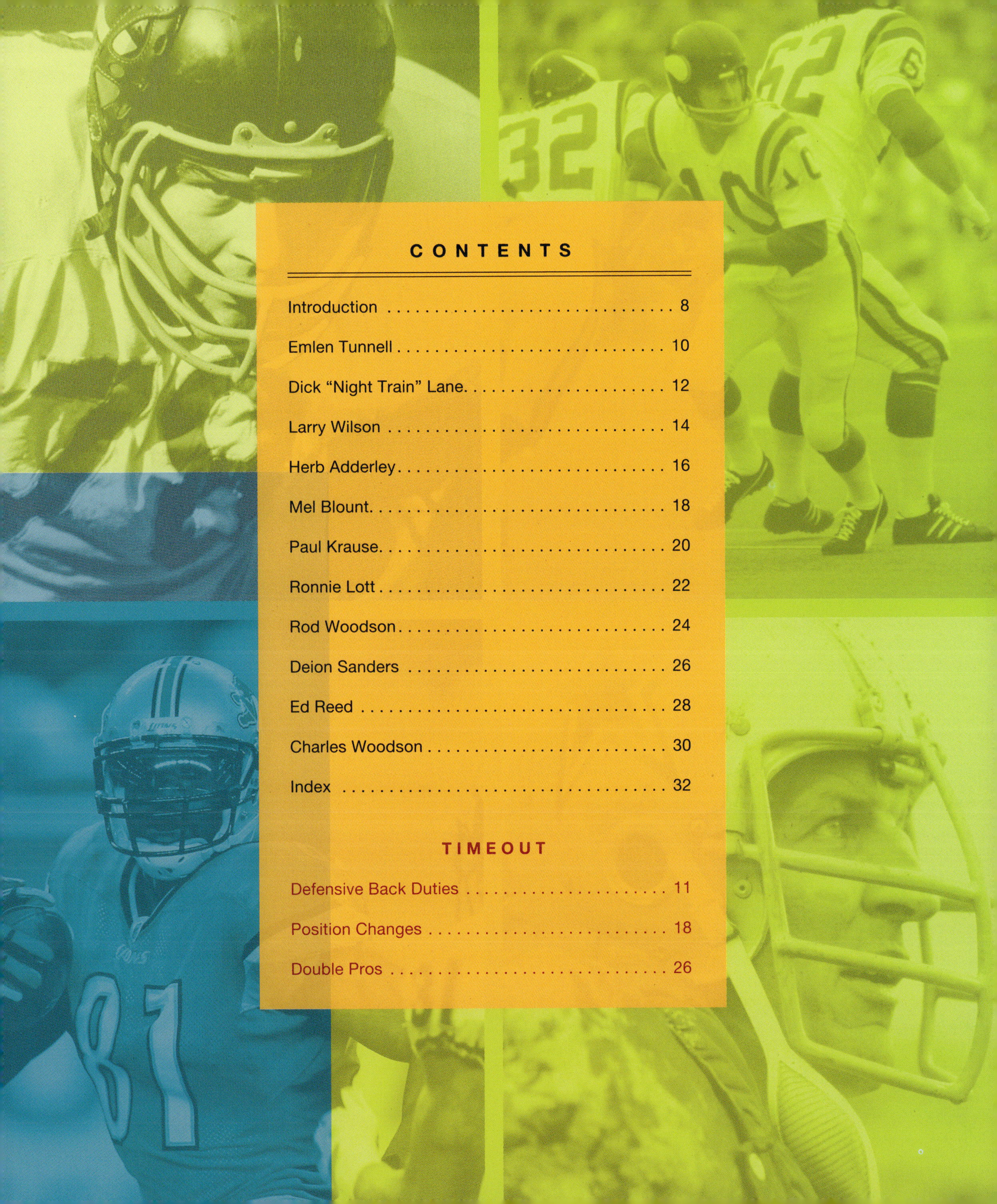

CONTENTS

TIMEOUT

INTRODUCTION

The Atlanta Falcons are driving deep into San Francisco 49ers territory. Falcons quarterback Jeff George drops back to pass. He throws toward the sideline. Intercepted! Deion Sanders, cornerback for the 49ers, high-steps 93 yards down the sideline for a defensive touchdown.

Cornerbacks and safeties make up football's defensive backfield. They are also called the secondary unit. Masters of seeing offensive moves before they happen, they are the last line of defense. They're fast, efficient tacklers. All defensive backs who play for the National Football League (NFL) are at the top of their game. But only a handful can be called Hall of Famers.

The Pro Football Hall of Fame honors 378 past players, coaches, and sport contributors. Of those, about 40 are defensive backs. This book highlights 11 Hall of Fame defensive backs whose careers reached above and beyond. This list isn't a ranking. Players are ordered by the year they were enshrined.

Deion Sanders

EMLEN TUNNELL (1925–75)
SAFETY
NEW YORK GIANTS SEASONS: 1948–58; GREEN BAY PACKERS SEASONS: 1959–61
HALL OF FAME CLASS: 1967
AWARDS/HONORS: MEMBER OF NFL 50TH/100TH ANNIVERSARY TEAMS, 9X PRO BOWL, 6X FIRST TEAM ALL-PRO, 1950S NFL ALL-DECADE TEAM, 2X NFL CHAMPION

EMLEN TUNNELL

Emlen Tunnell was the first African American to be elected to the Pro Football Hall of Fame. He was the leader of a strong New York Giants secondary unit of the 1950s. He was a great defender and a great return specialist. When he retired following the 1961 season, Tunnell held the NFL record for career interceptions with 79. He held the record for punt return yards, too, with 2,209. Tunnell's interceptions still rank second all-time.

Before his NFL career began, Tunnell enlisted in the U.S. Coast Guard. He served during World War II (1939–45). He received a medal for heroism when he saved a shipmate from drowning.

Tunnell broke into the league in 1948. He made an impact right away. He intercepted 7 passes his first season and then picked off a career-high 10 in 1949. He returned three interceptions for touchdowns in his first two seasons. In 1951, Tunnell ran all across the field. He intercepted nine passes. He also returned three punts and one kickoff for touchdowns. His efforts in 1951 earned him the first of his six First Team All-Pro selections. Tunnell was selected to play in the Pro Bowl nine times in his career.

Tunnell intercepted six passes in 1956. He led the team to a beat-down 47–7 win over the Chicago Bears in the NFL Championship Game. It marked New York's first championship in 18 years. Tunnell played his last three seasons with the Green Bay Packers. In 1961, with Green Bay, he won his second NFL championship.

Emlen Tunnell (right)

DEFENSIVE BACK DUTIES

There are three lines of defense. Defensive backs are the last one. They cover wide receivers and tight ends. If a ball carrier gets through the first two lines of defense (defensive linemen, linebackers), it is the defensive backs' job to keep him out of the end zone. Defensive backs focus on pass coverage. They help with run support. Sometimes, they will rush the quarterback. Defensive backs are usually the quickest defenders. Cornerbacks cover the speedy wide receivers. Safeties cover wherever needed. Defensive backs must have great vision and the ability to anticipate moves.

DICK "NIGHT TRAIN" LANE

DICK "NIGHT TRAIN" LANE (1928–2002)
CORNERBACK
LOS ANGELES RAMS SEASONS: 1952–53; CHICAGO CARDINALS SEASONS: 1954–59; DETROIT LIONS SEASONS: 1960–65
HALL OF FAME CLASS: 1974
AWARDS/HONORS: MEMBER OF NFL 50TH/75TH/100TH ANNIVERSARY TEAMS, 7X PRO BOWL, 10X ALL-PRO (7X FIRST TEAM), 1950S NFL ALL-DECADE TEAM

There may not be another defensive player as gifted athletically as Dick Lane. He had the speed and agility to intercept passes anywhere. He also had the ability to deliver crushing tackles. Lane got his nickname, "Night Train," in his first year in the NFL. Every time the song "Night Train" played, Lane danced. The nickname stuck. "Night Train" derailed many opposing offenses. In his first season, he intercepted a league-high 14 passes in just 12 games. Two of them were returned for touchdowns. The 14 interceptions are a single-season NFL record that still stands as of 2024. Lane led the league again in interceptions in 1954 with 10. He returned interceptions for touchdowns in his career five times.

Lane received First or Second Team All-Pro honors every year from 1954 to 1963. He was also named to seven Pro Bowls. He earned all of these honors despite not playing years of college football before turning pro. Lane played one year of junior college football in Nebraska. Then he enlisted in the U.S. Army. He served four years. He was able to stay in "football shape" by playing on a military football team.

Lane was one of the most feared tacklers in football. He was known for his clothesline tackle. This tackle focuses on the head and neck area. It's no longer allowed in the game.

LARRY WILSON

LARRY WILSON (1938–2020)
SAFETY
ST. LOUIS CARDINALS SEASONS: 1960–72
HALL OF FAME CLASS: 1978
AWARDS/HONORS: MEMBER OF NFL 75TH/100TH ANNIVERSARY TEAMS, 8X PRO BOWL, 7X ALL-PRO (6X FIRST TEAM), 1960S/1970S NFL ALL-DECADE TEAMS, NFL DEFENSIVE PLAYER OF THE YEAR

Offenses do not suspect safeties, from the last line of defense, to rush the quarterback. The St. Louis Cardinals were one of the first teams to use this tactic. Larry Wilson was one of the first to excel in it. Many believe Wilson was the creator of the "safety blitz." It's a play where a safety rushes the quarterback right after the snap. Wilson "unofficially" tallied 21 sacks from his safety position over his 13-year career. (Sacks were not considered an official stat until 1982.)

Wilson was also great at intercepting passes. In 1966, he led the league with 10 interceptions, 2 of which he returned for touchdowns. He recorded at least one interception in seven straight games. That year he was named NFL Defensive Player of the Year by the Newspaper Enterprise Association. Wilson collected 52 interceptions over his career. He played in the Pro Bowl eight times. He was named All-Pro seven times, six times as First Team All-Pro.

Wilson was well known for his toughness. It didn't matter if he had broken bones. If he could run, he could play. Playing with broken wrists, Wilson once intercepted a pass with casts on both hands! He developed his toughness because scouts considered him to be too small. He was not selected until the seventh round of the 1960 NFL Draft. "You've only got 60 minutes to prove what kind of player you are," he said. "Forty-nine minutes aren't enough. You've got to give 100 percent on every play."

HERB ADDERLEY

HERB ADDERLEY (1939–2020)
CORNERBACK
GREEN BAY PACKERS SEASONS: 1961–69; DALLAS COWBOYS SEASONS: 1970–72
HALL OF FAME CLASS: 1980
AWARDS/HONORS: 5X PRO BOWL, 7X ALL-PRO (5X FIRST TEAM), 1960S NFL ALL-DECADE TEAM, 3X SUPER BOWL CHAMPION, 3X NFL CHAMPION

In college, Herb Adderley was an All-Big Ten selection. He played offense as a halfback at Michigan State University. He was a first-round selection in the 1961 NFL Draft by the Green Bay Packers. Green Bay already had two future Hall of Fame running backs on their roster. Getting regular playing time would be tough. Needing a cornerback later in the season, head coach Vince Lombardi switched Adderley to defense. It became the start of an amazing career. Adderley started only one game his rookie season. But from then on, he started regularly at cornerback. He intercepted seven passes in 1962, returning one for a touchdown. He earned the first of his five First Team All-Pro honors that season.

Adderley was a big part of winning teams. Half of his 12 seasons in the league ended with a championship. He was on three Super Bowl-winning teams (two with Green Bay and one with the Dallas Cowboys). He also won three NFL championships with Green Bay before the Super Bowl began. In Super Bowl II (2), following the 1967 season, Adderley returned an interception 60 yards for a game-clinching touchdown. It was the only interception return for a touchdown in the first 10 Super Bowls.

Adderley recorded 48 interceptions in his career. He returned seven of them for touchdowns, including a league-high three touchdowns in 1965. He made five straight Pro Bowls from 1963 to 1967. He intercepted five passes over 15 career playoff games, including two in the 1967 postseason.

No. 47 Mel Blount

POSITION CHANGES

In pro football's early days, defensive backs were allowed to make contact with receivers well downfield before the ball was thrown. That changed in 1978. Defensive backs now have only five yards from the line of scrimmage to make contact with a receiver downfield. If that contact is made beyond five yards, the defender gets a penalty. This rule is sometimes called the "Mel Blount Rule." Blount was known for maintaining contact on receivers well downfield.

MEL BLOUNT (1948–)
CORNERBACK
PITTSBURGH STEELERS SEASONS: 1970–83
HALL OF FAME CLASS: 1989
AWARDS/HONORS: MEMBER OF NFL 75TH/100TH ANNIVERSARY TEAMS, 5X PRO BOWL, 6X ALL-PRO (2X FIRST TEAM), 1980S NFL ALL-DECADE TEAM, NFL DEFENSIVE PLAYER OF THE YEAR, 4X SUPER BOWL CHAMPION

MEL BLOUNT

Mel Blount was the shut-down cornerback of the famed "Steel Curtain" defense of the 1970s. He is one of five Steelers defenders in the Pro Football Hall of Fame. Blount was a member of all four Super Bowl championship teams from the 1970s. His best season may have been 1975. He led the NFL in interceptions with 11. He was named NFL Defensive Player of the Year. That year was the second of Pittsburgh's four titles in the decade.

Blount played 14 years in the league. He recorded at least one interception every year. He was bigger and quicker than most cornerbacks during the 1970s. He used his size and speed to intercept 57 passes over his career. "Cornerback was a challenging position to play, but I felt there was nobody I couldn't cover," he said. "But there's one thing for sure—you had to have nerves of steel to play cornerback."

Blount was in top form in the playoffs. In the 1979 American Football Conference (AFC) Championship Game, his fumble recovery led to the winning touchdown. The win advanced Pittsburgh to Super Bowl XIV (14). A year earlier, his interception sparked a Steeler drive. The push led to a go-ahead touchdown in the Super Bowl XIII (13) victory over the Dallas Cowboys. Blount had five Pro Bowl nods over his career. He was named to six All-Pro Teams with two First Team honors.

PAUL KRAUSE

PAUL KRAUSE (1942–)
SAFETY
WASHINGTON REDSKINS SEASONS: 1964–67; MINNESOTA VIKINGS SEASONS: 1968–79
HALL OF FAME CLASS: 1998
AWARDS/HONORS: 8X PRO BOWL, 6X ALL-PRO (3X FIRST TEAM), NFL CAREER INTERCEPTIONS LEADER

Paul Krause had one of the best defensive rookie seasons in NFL history. He was selected in the second round of the 1964 NFL Draft by the Washington Redskins. Quarterbacks learned right away that they did not want to throw the ball Krause's way. He intercepted 12 passes to lead the league in 1964. He was runner-up in voting for NFL Rookie of the Year. He made the first of his eight Pro Bowls and was named First Team All-Pro. Krause intercepted 16 more passes over the next three seasons, including 8 in 1967. Despite the success, Krause was traded to the Minnesota Vikings in 1968. He would continue to add to his interception total wearing purple.

The Vikings defense of the 1970s was led by the "Purple People Eaters." That was the nickname for the team's defensive line. Minnesota made four Super Bowl appearances during Krause's 12 years with the Vikings. Unfortunately, they lost each game. It was not because of Krause, though. He made an interception in one game and recovered a fumble in another.

Krause's best season with Minnesota may have been 1975. He collected 10 interceptions for a league-high 201 return yards. He earned the final First Team All-Pro and Pro Bowl nods of his career. "I'm plain and simple the safety man, the guy who has to stop the play when the others don't, and that's the way I like it," he said.

22

RONNIE LOTT

RONNIE LOTT (1959–)
CORNERBACK/SAFETY
SAN FRANCISCO 49ERS SEASONS: 1981–90; LOS ANGELES RAIDERS SEASONS: 1991–92; NEW YORK JETS SEASONS: 1993–94
HALL OF FAME CLASS: 2000
AWARDS/HONORS: MEMBER OF NFL 75TH/100TH ANNIVERSARY TEAMS, 10X PRO BOWL, 8X FIRST TEAM ALL-PRO, 1980S/1990S NFL ALL-DECADE TEAMS, 4X SUPER BOWL CHAMPION

Ronnie Lott made an immediate impact on the San Francisco 49ers after he was picked in the first round of the 1981 NFL Draft. Lott brought a winning mindset with him. He had won a national championship playing at the University of Southern California. The 49ers had missed the playoffs eight straight years prior to Lott's arrival. In 1981, San Francisco finished with a 13–3 record. Starting at cornerback for all 16 games, Lott intercepted 7 passes. He returned three of them for touchdowns. He was runner-up for NFL Defensive Player of the Year. He made the first of 10 Pro Bowl teams and was named First Team All-Pro. Best of all, he helped the 49ers win their first Super Bowl. And he was just getting started.

Lott helped San Francisco win another Super Bowl title in 1984. Two more Super Bowl wins came after the 1988 and 1989 seasons. Lott was one of only five players who were on all four 49ers championship teams of the 1980s. He continued to be a fierce presence. In 1986, he led the league with 10 interceptions. Lott signed with the Los Angeles Raiders in 1991. In his first season with the silver and black, he once again led the league in interceptions, with eight. He collected 63 interceptions over his 14-year career, returning 5 for touchdowns.

The Lott IMPACT Trophy was created in 2004. It is presented each season to college football's defensive IMPACT player of the year. IMPACT stands for integrity, maturity, performance, academics, community, and tenacity.

ROD WOODSON

ROD WOODSON (1965–)
CORNERBACK/SAFETY
PITTSBURGH STEELERS SEASONS: 1987–96; SAN FRANCISCO 49ERS SEASON: 1997; BALTIMORE RAVENS SEASONS: 1998–2001; OAKLAND RAIDERS SEASONS: 2002–03
HALL OF FAME CLASS: 2009
AWARDS/HONORS: MEMBER OF NFL 75TH/100TH ANNIVERSARY TEAMS, 11X PRO BOWL, 9X ALL-PRO (6X FIRST TEAM), 1990S NFL ALL-DECADE TEAM, NFL DEFENSIVE PLAYER OF THE YEAR, SUPER BOWL CHAMPION

Rod Woodson was a versatile player at Purdue University. He played offense, defense, and returned punts and kickoffs. The Pittsburgh Steelers selected the "triple threat" in the first round of the 1987 NFL Draft. With the Steelers, Woodson became a "dual threat." He starred on defense at the cornerback position and on special teams. He would return four punts/kickoffs for touchdowns in his career. But it was on defense where he earned his acclaim. He collected 71 interceptions over his 17-year career, good for third all-time. He returned 12 of them for touchdowns—an NFL record.

Woodson received his first Pro Bowl and First Team All-Pro nods in 1989. He later added 11 more Pro Bowl nods and nine First or Second Team All-Pro honors. In 1993, Woodson set a career high with eight interceptions. He did it all defensively that season. He led the team with 79 solo tackles. He also recorded 28 passes defensed, forced two fumbles, and had two quarterback sacks. For his efforts, he was named NFL Defensive Player of the Year.

Woodson changed teams and positions later in his career. He joined the Baltimore Ravens in 1999, playing safety. In 2000, he was a member of one of the greatest defenses of all time. The Ravens set an NFL record for fewest points allowed in a 16-game season. They went on to win Super Bowl XXXV (35).

DOUBLE PROS

Fewer than 70 athletes have played both Major League Baseball (MLB) and in the National Football League (NFL). Only seven have done so since 1970. Only two from that list played both sports in the same year: Bo Jackson and Deion Sanders. Jackson played for three MLB teams from 1986 to 1994 and for the Los Angeles Raiders from 1987 to 1990. He is the only athlete to have been selected as an All-Star in both leagues.

DEION SANDERS

DEION SANDERS (1967–)
CORNERBACK
ATLANTA FALCONS SEASONS: 1989–93; SAN FRANCISCO 49ERS SEASON: 1994; DALLAS COWBOYS SEASONS: 1995–99; WASHINGTON REDSKINS SEASON: 2000; BALTIMORE RAVENS SEASONS: 2004–05
HALL OF FAME CLASS: 2011
AWARDS/HONORS: MEMBER OF NFL 100TH ANNIVERSARY TEAM, 8X PRO BOWL, 8X ALL-PRO (6X FIRST TEAM), 1990S NFL ALL-DECADE TEAM, NFL DEFENSIVE PLAYER OF THE YEAR, 2X SUPER BOWL CHAMPION

Deion Sanders is not only one of the greatest football players of all time but also one of the greatest athletes of all time. He played 14 years in the NFL and 9 years in Major League Baseball (MLB). With the MLB Atlanta Braves, Sanders led all of baseball in triples. He is the only athlete to play in both the Super Bowl and the World Series.

Nicknamed "Prime Time," Sanders was a threat every time he hit the football field. In his first NFL game, he returned a punt 68 yards for an Atlanta Falcons touchdown. At the end of the return, he high-stepped into the end zone. On defense, Sanders was well known as a "shut-down corner." Offenses tried to stay away from his side of the field. When they did throw his way, Sanders either knocked away passes or intercepted them. He intercepted 24 passes over his five years with Atlanta.

Sanders played with the San Francisco 49ers in 1994. There, he intercepted six passes, returning three for touchdowns. He was named NFL Defensive Player of the Year as the 49ers won the Super Bowl. He went on to play for the Dallas Cowboys the next season and won his second straight Super Bowl title. With the Cowboys, he became more of an offensive threat. In addition to cornerback, Sanders played wide receiver. He caught 36 passes in 1996.

After his playing career, Sanders spent time in broadcasting and later in coaching. He is now the head football coach at the University of Colorado.

ED REED

ED REED (1978–)
SAFETY
BALTIMORE RAVENS SEASONS: 2002–12; HOUSTON TEXANS SEASON: 2013; NEW YORK JETS SEASON: 2013
HALL OF FAME CLASS: 2019
AWARDS/HONORS: MEMBER OF NFL 100TH ANNIVERSARY TEAM, 9X PRO BOWL, 8X ALL-PRO (5X FIRST TEAM), 2000S NFL ALL-DECADE TEAM, NFL DEFENSIVE PLAYER OF THE YEAR, SUPER BOWL CHAMPION

Ed Reed is one of the most accomplished safeties in NFL history. Reed was selected by the Baltimore Ravens in the first round of the 2002 NFL Draft. Two years prior, the Ravens won the Super Bowl with one of the strongest defenses of all time. Making an early impression would be tough. Reed was up to the task. He earned a starting spot for the regular season. He started all 16 games and intercepted 5 passes. He would pick off a lot more passes over his 12-year career. Three times he led the league in interceptions. No other player in NFL history has accomplished that feat.

Reed holds three other NFL records. He collected 1,590 interception return yards off his 64 career interceptions. The return yardage was aided by the two longest interception returns in NFL history, both held by Reed. He returned an NFL-record 106 yards for a touchdown in 2004. In 2008, he topped that by one yard, going 107 yards for a score. Reed excels in postseason play, too. He played on seven Ravens teams that reached the postseason. He intercepted nine playoff passes, tied for the most in NFL history. In his last season in Baltimore, Reed intercepted a pass in Super Bowl XLVII (47). It helped the Ravens win their second Super Bowl title.

One of Reed's best seasons came in 2004. He led the league in interceptions for the first time, with nine. He was named NFL Defensive Player of the Year.

PACKERS
21
21
Riddell

CHARLES WOODSON

CHARLES WOODSON (1976–)
CORNERBACK/SAFETY
OAKLAND RAIDERS SEASONS: 1998–2005, 2013–15; GREEN BAY PACKERS SEASONS: 2006–12
HALL OF FAME CLASS: 2021
AWARDS/HONORS: 9X PRO BOWL, 8X ALL-PRO (4X FIRST TEAM), 2000S NFL ALL-DECADE TEAM, NFL DEFENSIVE PLAYER OF THE YEAR, NFL DEFENSIVE ROOKIE OF THE YEAR, SUPER BOWL CHAMPION

Even before Charles Woodson played an NFL game, he was already well known for his football talents. In 1997, while playing at the University of Michigan, he became the only primarily defensive player to win the Heisman Trophy. The award is given to the best college football player of the season. Woodson had helped Michigan win the national championship. The Oakland Raiders selected Woodson with the fourth overall pick in the 1998 NFL Draft. He would prove his talents at the pro level. He started all 16 games for the Raiders that year. He intercepted five passes, returning one for a touchdown. He was named NFL Defensive Rookie of the Year.

Woodson was on a Raiders team that reached the Super Bowl following the 2002 season. He largely played on losing teams, though, in Oakland. He signed with the Green Bay Packers in 2006. His career blossomed. He intercepted eight passes in his first season in Green Bay. He led the league with nine interceptions in 2009. He returned three of those for touchdowns. Woodson was named NFL Defensive Player of the Year. The following year, he helped Green Bay win Super Bowl XLV (45). In 2011, he led the league in interceptions again, with seven.

Woodson returned to Oakland to play the last three seasons of his career. He became the first player in NFL history to collect at least 50 career interceptions and 20 career sacks. His 65 career interceptions are tied for fifth all-time.

INDEX